TENNIS
ENCYCLOPEDIA
FOR KIDS

Tennis Encyclopedia for Kids. Cooolz Ltd., 2019. 40 p., illustrated.

ISBN 978-9934-8711-6-0

Dear friends,

You are about to make a trip into the exciting world of tennis.

You will learn how the game developed, beginning in ancient times and continuing until today. You will learn its concept and rules. You will get to know the tennis court, racket, and ball. You will see why tennis is loved by millions of people.

You may think, "Why not learn to play tennis?" You will be right because tennis trains both the body and mind.

And it is cool!

Let's look back into the Stone Age and imagine what it was like. What did people have when they hardly had anything at all? There were no phones, no cars, no airplanes, and no internet. But the cave people had their own games and entertainment, and they also had a desire to compete with each other, and to win!

For example, in Fontanet Cave in France, scientists discovered the imprints of a clay ball hitting the floor almost 14,000 years ago!

In those ancient times, childhood passed faster than a pterodactyl could fly. As soon as boys reached the age of 12, they started making tools and hunting mammoths together with the adults. The ancient man spent most of his time swinging a cudgel. His swing had to be strong, which would be good for a future tennis player.

Though archaeologists kept finding ancient balls around the world, no one knows where the first game of tennis took place. One of the most ancient balls was found in a pharaoh's tomb in Egypt. The Egyptians had a religious team game in which every team played the match not for themselves but in the name of gods they represented.

In Ancient Greece, Rome, and Egypt, a ball was not just a simple toy. It was more than loved; it was venerated.

The Ancient Greeks believed a ball was a perfect object because it had the shape of the sun and therefore carried the same magic power.

For this reason, ball games were not played for fun. They were sacred rituals. By the way, the first Olympic games were also intended to please the gods.

Greeks sewed leather pieces into balls and stuffed them with straw, feathers, and moss. Then they discovered how to inflate it. In Greek, the ball was called **follis**. Big **follises** were used to play a game similar to football, and the small ones were for hand games similar to today's tennis.

Famous for their curiosity, Romans borrowed the idea of the ball from the Greeks, as they had borrowed many other ideas. Their **harpastum** game was part of legionary military training.

Bellicose (warlike) Romans spread ball activities around "with fire and sword".

Some cultures still use the "old recipe" balls. In the first days of spring, Japanese children play with **temari** balls to commemorate the times when the ball was a symbol of the sun.

A game vaguely resembling the tennis we know today was first mentioned in the 11th to 12th centuries.

In French monasteries, monks played a game that involved hitting a ball with their palms. The game was called **Jeu de Paume**, which translated from French means "the game of hand". Because it was quite painful to hit the ball with a bare palm, eventually special gloves and then wooden paddles strung with cow gut were used.

Jeu de Paume could be played by up to twelve people at the same time.

In the 12th century, one week before Easter each year, the bishop gave presents to his parish; on Easter day, they brought him their reciprocal gift, which was a set of tennis balls.

During the game, players would scream out, "Catch it!" Some people believe that the word **tennis** actually came from the French verb **tenez**, meaning "to hold", although it is still unknown exactly when **Jeu de Paume** was renamed tennis.

By the 15th to 16th centuries, the game spread beyond the monasteries and became popular around France.

Ropes were strung across the narrow streets so people could paddle the ball back and forth. The balls rattled around, bouncing against the stone pavement to the delight of spectators. It was very noisy and a lot of fun. Even back then, tennis gathered crowds of fans.

The popularity of the game is proven by the fact that there were thirty craftsmen in Paris whose speciality was ball making. Is that many specialists or not? Let's compare: One paint supplier was enough in order to paint the entire city of Paris.

The people living in the backstreets of Paris were not the only people to be enthralled by the game; tennis became part of everyday life in royal palaces and noblemens' castles. To hide from prying eyes, regal players built indoor courts with galleries for selected spectators.

There were many tennis lovers among the French kings:

Louis X was quite a good tennis player.

Louis XI issued a decree regulating ball-making. His daughter Anne de Beaujeu played tennis since childhood, which was very unusual for a lady.

Charles V built two playing halls, one of them being in the Louvre, where the French kings lived at that time.

Another outstanding player was Charles of Orléans. During the Hundred Years' War, the English captured him and kept him as a prisoner of war for twenty years. Interestingly, his captors allowed him to play his favorite game every day.

The Duke of Orléans taught the English King Henry V to play tennis.

Among all the French kings, Henry IV was the biggest fan of tennis. He played it whenever he had time and even issued a decree to formulate tennis rules.

When the Duke of Orléans taught Henry V to play tennis, the tennis boom reached England. Henry V was the first of the English royals to become interested in tennis. He played the game on a regular basis. This was described by William Shakespeare in his play **Henry V**. In the play, in 1415 during the Hundred Years' War, Henry V received a chest of tennis balls from the French dauphin. Henry V took the gesture as a reminder of the "wilder days" of his youth when he loved playing tennis. He saw it as a provocative, insulting act in the context of the interrupted peaceful negotiations. As a result, Henry V set off to France to take his revenge on the battlefield. Of course, it is just a literary plot and unproven by any historical documents.

However, it is known that during the Hundred Years' War, negotiations could take place right on the tennis court. One of these "international tournaments" was held between Henry VIII and Francis I, two passionate players. The game lasted for seven days with no clear advantage on either side.

Despite the time taken, the game did not change anything in the history of the countries; the war was not over.

Henry VIII played a very important role in the history of English tennis. During his reign, the game reached its golden period. One of the tennis courts built by Henry VIII, Hampton Court, is still used by local club members. The English referred to the game played at that time as real tennis. Why? Because by that time, the simple game played for fun had developed into a serious competition where real bets on the winners were placed.

February 24, 1874, is tennis's unofficial birthday.

On this day, the enterprising Englishman Walter Clopton Wingfield was awarded Letters Patent No. 685, "A Portable Court for Playing Tennis." He also invented the tennis lawn and developed the rules of the game he later called **Sphairistiké** (from the Greek "**ball games**").

However, this name was a little complicated, and over time the game became known as lawn tennis.

Playing on the lawn became possible due to the invention of the rubber ball, which could bounce high on the grass.

Walter Wingfield started selling tennis kits and tennis rules books, but soon the popular game got out of his control.

When too many competitors appeared in 1877, Wingfield refused to extend the patent.

In the meanwhile, the game was rapidly conquering new countries: the United States, India, China, Canada, Australia, Russia, and, finally, the entire world.

In June 1877, The Field magazine announced the open lawn tennis championship at the All-England Club of **Wimbledon**. That was the first Wimbledon tournament: twenty-two participants and 200 spectators. That first year, the championship was a men's singles tournament; in 1884, the women's tournament was organized. The project proved to be successful, and the tournament has been held at Wimbledon held every summer since. The Wimbledon tournament has millions of fans. Eighty TV companies broadcast the game worldwide.

In the late 19th century, another prestigious championship appeared. A wealthy collegian and member of the Harvard tennis team, Dwight Filley Davis, invited his British friends for holidays and came up with the idea of a match against the Boston team. He prepared a surprise for the participants: a silver cup weighing over 6 kilograms.

After that, the tennis associations of Great Britain and the U.S.A. decided to hold an annual tournament between their national teams. Since 1900, the winner is awarded a perpetual trophy, the **Davis Cup**. As the years went by, other tennis tournaments, awards, and titles appeared.

The largest and the most prestigious ones are the **Grand Slam** tournaments: the Australian Open, Rolland Garros, the U.S. Open, and, of course, the famous Wimbledon tournament. The term **Grand Slam** was adopted in the 1930s from the bridge card game, where grand slam means absolute success. For a tennis player, winning all four tournaments in a single year means winning the grand slam, though the winner does not get a cup, statuette, or any other physical symbol of success. But they win the title every tennis player aspires to achieve.

We have learnt so much about tennis, and we can't wait to get to the court!

Tennis is a great way to have fun with your friends. Tennis is cool!

However, apart from having fun, there are many other reasons to pick up a racket.

First of all, tennis trains your body.

Second, tennis develops your mind.

Training improves your stamina, which helps you be successful in all spheres of life. Champions are made, not born; training is the only way for an athlete to succeed.

Every beginner usually asks, "Can I do that?" Of course you can! Any hobby begins with a wish. Who knows, maybe you will write your name in the history of tennis.

But there are many other things you need to know before you start playing. Where to play? What to play with? How to play?

Let's learn more!

To begin with, let's figure out how the game is played.

Tennis is played by the opponents standing on opposite sides of the court, using rackets to hit a ball over a net.

If the game is played by two players, one on each side of the court, it is a singles match.

If it is played by two players on each side of the court, it is a doubles match.

To make the game more challenging, several restrictions were introduced.

The ball must be returned before it touches the court surface or after the first bounce. The ball must fly over the net without grazing it.

On the opposite side of the court, the ball must hit the court within the marked boundaries.

The serve is judged good if the ball lands in the inner box over the net and diagonally across from the server.

The main task of every player is to hit the ball in such a way that the opponent cannot return it.

Tennis is played on a rectangular field called the **court**. It is 78 feet (23,78 meters) long and 27 feet (8,23 meters) wide.

The field of play is marked with lines and divided into two parts by a **net**.

The lines along the short sides of the court are called **baselines**, and the lines along the long sides are called **sidelines**.

The **service line** marks the back edge of the service boxes and lies between the net and the baseline. The area between the service line and the baseline is called the **backcourt**.

Competition courts have umpire chairs and stands for spectators. For example, the Davis Cup has a minimum capacity of 12,000 seats in the stands.

There are different kinds of court: grass, clay (usually orange but sometimes dark green), hard, synthetic carpet, asphalt, acrylic, concrete, or wooden. The court is designed for the comfort of athletes. The floor is perfectly smooth and springy. The ball bounces well, and the the players' shoes do not slip. The court is arranged in such a way that the sun never gets in the eyes of the players. The court is carefully maintained. Before the game, it is rinsed with water and leveled with a special drag. If there are any scratches or uneven areas, they are backfilled with a specific mix.

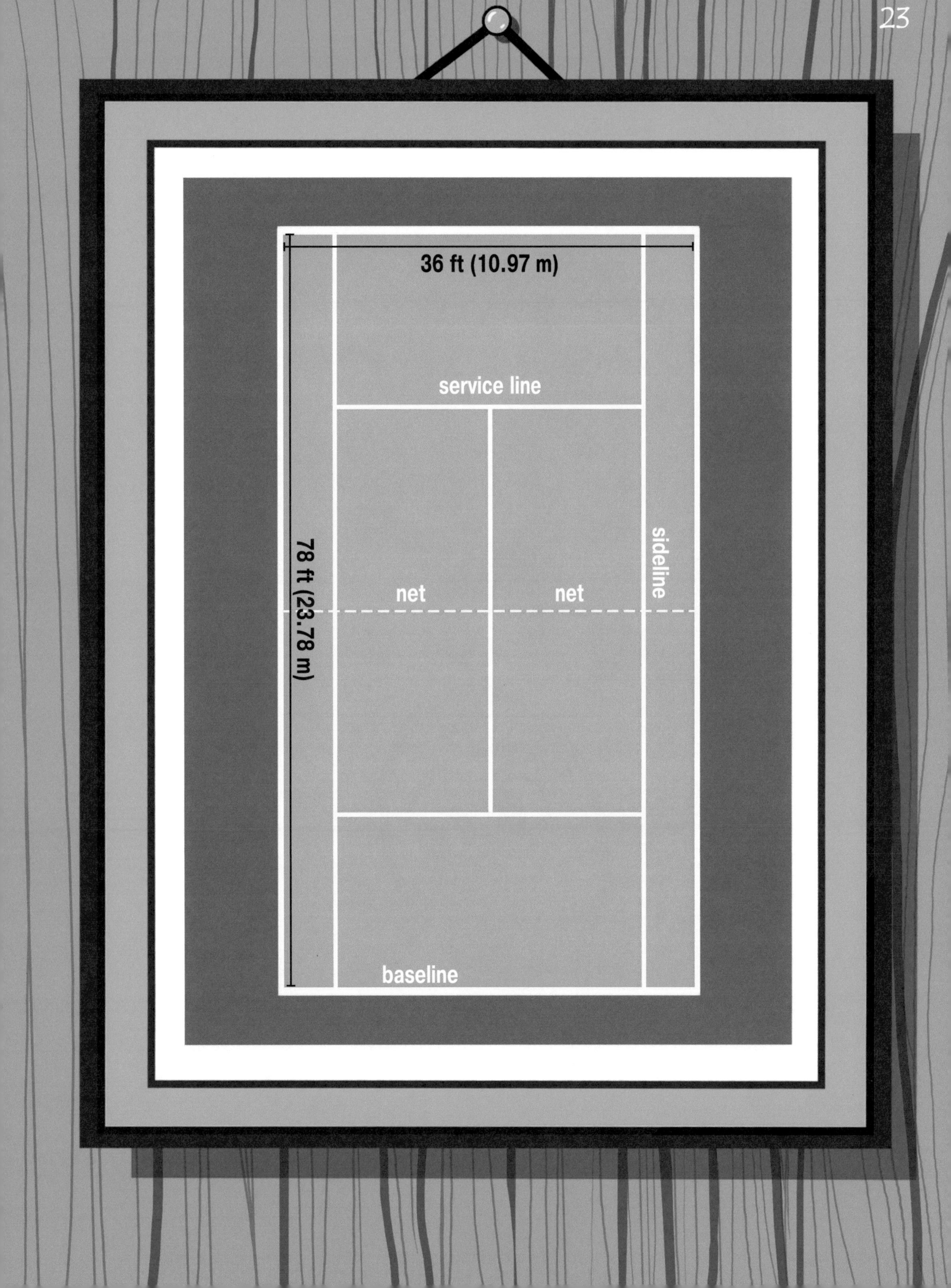

36 ft (10.97 m)

service line

78 ft (23.78 m)

net

net

sideline

baseline

The first rackets were made of wood, and the strings were animal guts.

The first amendments to the racket took place in the 1960s. Large racket-producing companies began experimenting with the size and shape of rackets to improve their strength, speed, and accuracy of strokes.

In 1953, René Lacoste patented the first metal racket. After that, rackets were produced from aluminum, graphite, fiberglass, or carbon fiber.

Today's athletes normally use graphite rackets because graphite is a strong but lightweight material.

Metal rackets are mostly produced for children and amateurs.

Racket performance depends on its hardness, weight, and handle size. Tennis rules include requirements for professional rackets, including their length, size, and arrangement of strings.

Tennis players choose rackets based on their level of skill and playing style. The racket must be comfortable.

Coaches normally recommend that children under the age of ten play with light, shortened rackets with thinner handles, because this makes it easier to hit the ball and to train the stroke technique. How do you choose the right racket for your height? Stand up straight, hold the racket, and lower your hand toward the floor. If the distance between the top of the racket and the floor is 1.98 inches (5 centimeters), it is the right size for you.

The first tennis balls were made of sheep stomachs and leather, stuffed with chalk, sand, and sawdust.

In 1870, rubber was invented, which turned out to be perfect for making light and bouncy balls. To make the balls more resistant, they were coated with a fibrous felt covering.

The felt-coated rubber balls production technology has survived until current times.

The traditional white line around the ball dates back to the 18th century. In those times, balls were held together with white threads.

A modern tennis ball must conform to the established requirements for weight (1.98–2.10 ounces [56.0–59.4 grams]) and size (2.57–2.70 inches [6.54–6.86 centimetres]). The bright yellow ball is easy to see on the TV screen, which is why white balls are hardly ever used.

Every day, an enormous number of balls is produced.

Just imagine 300 million per year!

The balls wear out very quickly, producing 15,000 tons of scrap rubber.

To solve the waste disposal problem in the United States, it is common practice to repair the balls after a tournament.

These renovated balls are donated to tennis organizations.

An unusual ball-recycling solution was found in England. After large tournaments, the bright felt is removed from the ball, and its core becomes a cozy home for field mice. Do you think the mice are happy?

As with any other game, tennis has rules that must be observed by both athletes and amateurs.

The game consists of sets; sets are divided into games. In every game, points are scored.

The game begins with a serve. The players have two chances to land their ball into the service box. If the serve fails, the point is lost.

Whoever serves first continues to serve until that game is over. Then it is the other player's turn to serve.

Tennis owes its scoring system to the French monks based on 15-30-45 (quarters of an hour on a clock face). Over time, 45 became 40.

Therefore, the score increments to 40 points.

For the first two successful serves, 15 points are scored; for the third one, 10 points are scored.

Three successful serves in a row makes 15 + 15 + 10 = 40.

Once you win the fourth serve, you win the game.

If each player has scored 40 points, the score is called **deuce**, which is translated as equal (from the French **deux le jeu**, meaning "equal score at this point of the game").

After deuce, the players fight for the advantage, not the points.

Once the game is tied, you need to win two serves in a row.

The set continues until one player has won six games.

If the score is 5:5, you have to win seven games rather than five.

When the game is tied at 6:6, the game has a tie-break.

In the tie-break, a player gets one point for every serve they win.

To win, you need to score seven points. If the score gets to 6:6 in a tie-break, you must have a two point advantage to win.

Usually a match consists of three sets. To win the match, you need to win two sets.

At the most prestigious men's tournaments, matches are played until one player has three victories in five sets.

Now let's get to know the contemporary games related to lawn tennis. They have a ball, a racket, and a field in common.

The Spanish love playing **padel** tennis. It is also well known in other European countries and in America. How does it look? The court is similar to that of tennis but smaller. The net is lower, and the racket is shorter. The main difference is that the court is surrounded by transparent walls; the ball may bounce both from the floor and the walls. The scoring system is the same as in lawn tennis.

According to the rules, padel tennis is played by doubles, but singles games are also possible. Padel tennis is open to everyone and can be played even by a beginner.

Another relative of tennis is table tennis, or **ping-pong**. The name originated from the distinctive sound the ball produces as it bounces off the table.

Ping-pong was invented in England. Now it is played on all continents, but it is most popular in China.

The playing field for ping-pong is a table with a net. You can play singles or doubles. The rules are simple. To win the game, you need to score eleven points. After every game, the players switch sides. A full match consists of seven games, but there may be fewer. The match continues until one of the players wins four games.

Ping-pong is a popular and affordable kind of sport, needing only two paddles and a light plastic ball, but the pleasure of the game is immense.

Tennis players have always attracted the attention of the audience not only with their playing technique but also their clothing. In the history of tennis, the court has seen many fashion lovers. The tennis outfit has not always been short skirts, dresses, elegant polo shirts, and shorts.

For a long time, men wore long-sleeved shirts and trousers. When it was cold, they also wore a black sweater on top. The tennis clothes looked conservative, but at least it did not hinder movement. For the ladies, however, it must have been really uncomfortable running around the court in corset bodices and long dresses. Imagine playing tennis while wearing a hat that could fly away at any moment.

Suzanne Rachel Flore Lenglen changed all that. In 1922, the brave French girl walked onto the court in a sleeveless top, a knee-length skirt, and a bandana on her head to hold her hair back.

In the 1940s, trousers replaced shorts. T-shirts and shorts became a common outfit for both men and women. Ten years later, the American tennis player Gertrude Moran set the trend for the miniskirt. That was a scandal. Ted Tinling, who designed the outfit, was shunned for thirty-three years, but it didn't stop him. The designer continued his work. Thanks to him, women play tennis in the clothes we know today.

The contemporary men's outfit consists of a polo shirt or a crew neck shirt and tennis shorts. A usual women's attire is a fitted shirt with or without sleeves and a short skirt or a one-piece dress. Wrist bands, bandanas, visors, and hats are important accessories. Women playing tennis today pay a lot of attention to how they look.

Tennis footwear is selected depending on the court type. The shoes must be comfortable and wear-resistant and provide good friction without damaging the court.

Very often we hear athletes say, "Tennis is more than a sport to me; it is my lifestyle." But what does that mean? What is a lifestyle?

A lifestyle is the way of life you enjoy: who you spend your time with, what you dream about, what you do, and what you find interesting. For instance, one person may love sports and another prefers videogames. Someone may enjoy spending time with friends and someone else is a solitary couch potato. These are examples of different lifestyles.

How do tennis players live? They work hard and often on the court and they take care of their health so they can continue to play. They set goals and work toward achieving them. They communicate with people who share their interests and exchange experiences with them. They tend to be broad-minded because they travel a lot; there are so many amazing places in the world to see!

But the most important thing for a tennis player is to believe that your dreams may come true if you work hard. Be brave, think positive, and keep the good vibes! Live it in tennis style! Join us!

Color it!

CONTENTS

Tennis Encyclopedia for Kids.

Cooolz Ltd., 2019. 40 p., illustrated.

ISBN 978-9934-8711-6-0

ec32c23e-0451-4b2c-917d-5a758bacc1b5R01